All Shining in the Spring

THE STORY OF A BABY WHO DIED

SIOBHÁN PARKINSON

Illustrated by Donald Teskey

ALL SHINING IN THE SPRING

First published in 1995 by The O'Brien Press Ltd, Dublin, Ireland
This edition first published in 2021 by
Little Island Books
7 Kenilworth Park
Dublin 6w,
Ireland

First published in the USA in 2022

© Siobhán Parkinson 1995

All rights reserved. No part of this book may be reproduced, transmitted or stored in a retrieval system in any form or by any means (including electronic/digital, mechanical, photocopying, scanning, recording or otherwise, by means now known or hereinafter invented) without prior permission in writing from the publisher.

A British Library Cataloguing in Publication record for this book is available from the British Library.

Illustrated by Donald Teskey
Typeseting and cover design by Catherine Gaffney
Printed in Poland by L&C

Print ISBN: 978-1-91507-119-4

Little Island has received funding to support this book from the Arts Council of Ireland / An Chomhairle Ealaíon

10 9 8 7 6 5 4 3 2 1

A Note for Parents

This is a true story. It happened to me and my family. It was a long time ago now, but it is a story that still happens in families everywhere. Fortunately, not so many babies die these days but it does happen, and a high proportion of women experience a miscarriage at some time in their lives. For families who lose a baby the experience is very painful, for the siblings as well as for the parents.

Miscarriage, stillbirth and the death of a baby are not topics people like to discuss, and most people are especially reluctant to talk to small children about such sad events. But children can be as much affected by these things as their parents. Children may be frightened as well as sad and upset, and their own grief and fear may be compounded by worry for their parents.

That is why I wrote this book for my own son when he was small and trying to learn how to grieve his baby brother. I hope this book will help families affected by the death of a baby to open up a conversation with their children. I have striven not to offer empty reassurances and false hopes, but to tell the story simply and truthfully.

This book is meant to be read with a parent or trusted adult. It is probably a good idea for the adult to read the book first before introducing it to a child.

Children not directly affected by the death of a sibling may come into contact with families where such an event has occurred, and their parents also may find this book helpful.

For more information about stillbirth, Sudden Infant Death Syndrome (SIDS), and miscarriage, and for some notes on how you can use this book with children or in a classroom, visit:

www.littleisland.ie/allshining

To Matthew

and in memory of Daniel

Matthew lived with his
mother and father
and his beautiful black cat Jack.

He had a doll called Bobby and a bear called Freddy Teddy and lots of other teddies and cuddly animals.

Matthew went to school,
and had lots of friends.

His friends all had brothers
and sisters.

But Matthew just had his mother
and his father
and his black cat Jack
and Bobby and Freddy
and his cuddly toys.

One day, there was a very exciting
piece of news.

Matthew's mother and father
told him that Matthew's mother
had a new baby growing inside her.

At last Matthew was going to have
a little brother or sister –
he didn't mind which.

Matthew's mother bought him a
special book
all about how babies grow inside
their mothers.

Every few days they would read
from the book
and look at the pictures
and wonder how big their baby was
and if it had eyebrows yet or
fingernails.

Matthew could feel the baby kicking and squirming inside his mother when he sat close to her.

But it takes a very long time
for a baby to grow
from a tiny egg into a little person,
so Matthew had to wait and wait
and plan and plan.

He was going to help with the
new baby.

He could run upstairs and get
a clean diaper
when the baby needed a change.

And then, when the baby got older,
he was going to teach it
to walk and talk,
and he was going to read stories
to the baby
when it got old enough to
understand.

But then, one day,
something very sad happened.

Matthew's mother went to see
her doctor
and the doctor was worried about
the baby.

It wasn't growing properly
like the babies in the pictures
in Matthew's book.

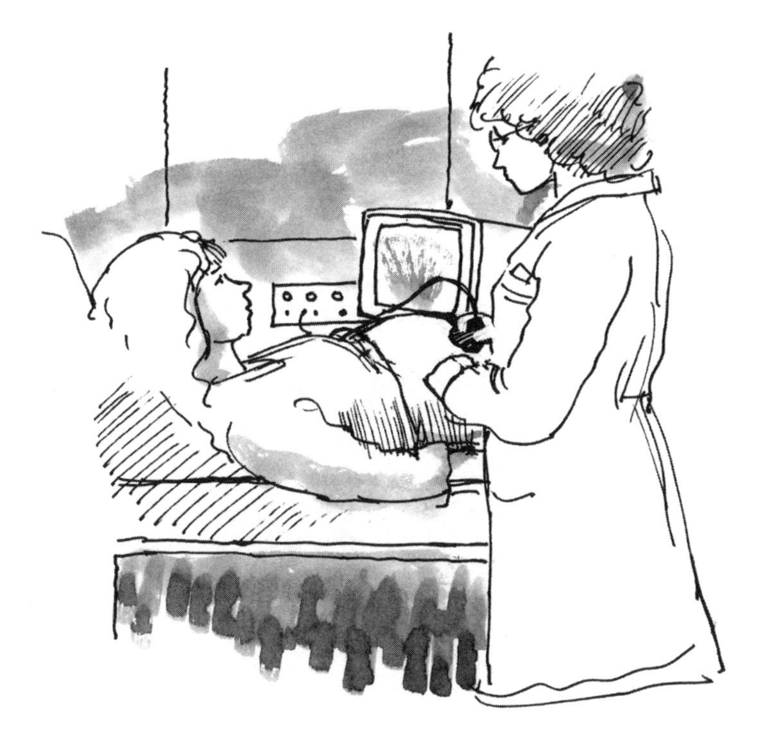

Matthew was very upset to hear that there was something wrong with his little brother or sister.

Every morning,
when he woke up,
he would come into
his parents' bedroom
and crawl into bed beside his mother
and stroke her big, round belly.

‘Poor baby,’ Matthew would say,
and give his mother’s belly a hug.

Matthew's mother and father
were sad too
because the baby wasn't
growing properly.

If it didn't grow properly
inside its mother,
then it wouldn't be strong
and healthy
when it was born.

'Is our baby going
to die?'
Matthew asked
his mother.

Matthew's
mother took
him on her knee
and she said that was right.
The baby wasn't going to be strong
enough to live outside her body.

Matthew was very, very sad
when he heard
that his brother or sister
wasn't going to live.

He cried a lot
and his mother cried
and his father cried.

His grandma and grandpa cried
and his other grandmother and
grandad cried too.
Everyone was sad.

‘It’s not fair that our baby
is going to die,’
said Matthew.
‘I thought only old people died.’

Matthew's mother and father
explained that of course
it is usually old people who die.
Their bodies get tired and worn out
and their life is over.

It's sad when an old person dies,
but you can remember
the fun you had with the old person
when they were strong and well,
and you know they have had
a good life.

But sometimes younger people
die too
if they get very ill
or if something is seriously wrong
with their bodies.

And even children can die
now and then.

Of course it is very unusual
for children to die.
Everyone knows that most children
are strong and healthy
and get well again
after they have been ill.

Most babies are strong and healthy too.

But some babies are fragile little people, and sometimes even tiny babies die.

Some babies die
while they are still growing
inside their mothers.

Some babies die at birth
or when they are still very,
very small.

And some babies die in their cot
when they are a few months old
and nobody quite knows why.

It's especially sad when a baby dies.

The baby hasn't had a good long life,
like an old person who dies.

And that seems unfair
and is hard to understand.

Matthew didn't understand
why his little brother or sister
was going to die,
and he felt all mixed up and cross
as well as sad and frightened.

He hugged his mother and father
when he felt like that,
and if they weren't there,
he just hugged Freddy Teddy.

The baby that was growing
inside Matthew's mother
was ready to be born now.

So Matthew's mother and father
went to the hospital for the birth.

Matthew didn't want
them to go to the
hospital and leave
him behind.

He was lonely and frightened,
even though he was with
his grandma.

But he knew that he wouldn't be
allowed to stay with his mother and
father in the hospital,
so he was very brave
and said goodbye to them.

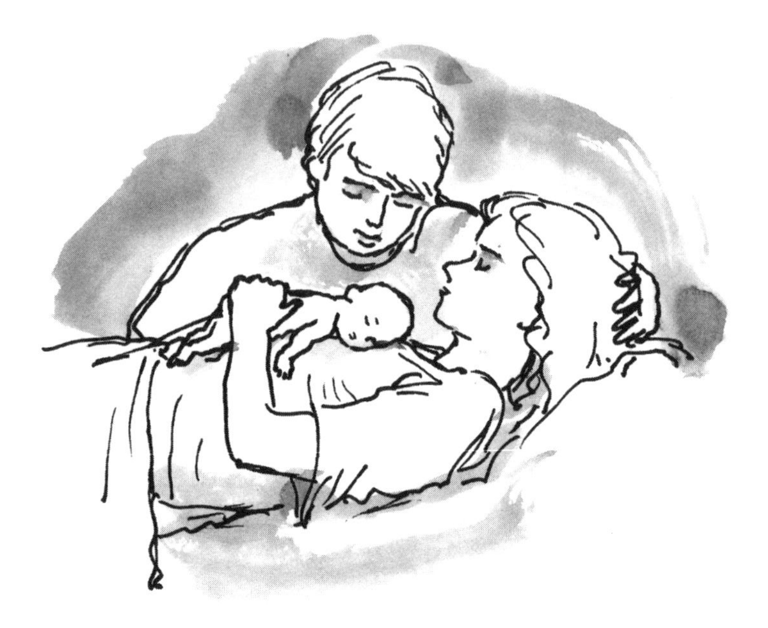

The baby was a little boy
and he was called Daniel.

He died right after he was born.

Matthew's mother held the baby
close to her,
and Matthew's father did the same.

They looked at their baby,
and they cried because he was dead.

As soon as he could,
Matthew and Daniel's father
brought Matthew to the hospital
to see his mother and the new baby.

Matthew was very sorry
that the baby was already dead.

'He's only a baby,' Matthew said to
his mother.
'He didn't even get a chance
to see you.'

He had a little cry
and his mother had a little cry.
They hugged each other very tightly,
and they both cried.

Matthew looked at his little brother,
lying in his tiny hospital cot.

Then he looked away again.

He didn't know whether
he wanted to look at Daniel
or whether he wanted to look away.

Daniel didn't look
quite like other babies.

His face was a bit blue
and squashed looking,
but his little body was perfect,
and he had lovely fingers and toes.

Matthew's mother and father
dressed baby Daniel all in white,
and they put his little body
into a pretty white coffin.

And then there was a service in
church, where everyone came
to say goodbye to Daniel.

Matthew sat in a seat
at the top of the church
between his mother and his father,
and held Freddy Teddy in his arms.

Freddy Teddy didn't understand
what was happening,
but Matthew knew
he was sad too.

There were flowers everywhere
and people talked
about how sad it was
that little Daniel hadn't had a chance
to grow up and have a life.

The coffin was taken away and buried in a special place, under the trees.

Matthew and his father went there shortly afterwards,
and they planted lots
of yellow flowers –
crocuses and daffodils and tulips.

'It will be all shining
when the spring comes,'
Matthew said.

When Matthew and his mother
and father
see the bright yellow flowers,
they remember Daniel.

They are still very sad
that they have no baby,
and when they feel sad,
they have a little cry.

Sometimes that makes
them feel better
and sometimes it doesn't.

But as time goes by,
Matthew and his mother and father
will not feel sad so often.

They will go to parties
and on picnics and on holidays,
and they will have good times
together.

But they will never forget
baby Daniel,

And no matter what happens,
he will always be Matthew's
little brother.

Acknowledgement

The author wishes to express her gratitude to The O'Brien Press, the first publishers of this book, for having the bravery and the foresight to publish it in the 1990s, and for their generosity in allowing it to be republished now, with the original illustrations by one of Ireland's finest artists, Donald Teskey.

About the Author

Siobhán Parkinson has written more than thirty books for children and adults. She was Ireland's first Laureate na nÓg (children's laureate). She is also a translator from German and she writes in Irish as well as in English. She lives in Dublin with her husband, the wood artist Roger Bennett.

All Shining in the Spring was her first book. It was in writing this book that Siobhán found her voice as a children's author, a gift she attributes to the baby she lost all those years ago.

About Little Island Books

Based in Dublin, Little Island Books has been publishing books for children and teenagers since 2010. It is Ireland's only English-language publisher that publishes exclusively for young people. Little Island specialises in publishing new Irish writers and illustrators, and also has a commitment to publishing books in translation.